Johnny Appleseed

For my son Jon, who is traveling the world and
planting good things —J. K.

For Scott and Fiona with many thanks —M. H.

First Aladdin edition September 2004

Text copyright © 2004 by Jane Kurtz
Illustrations copyright © 2004 by Mary Haverfield

ALADDIN PAPERBACKS
An imprint of Simon & Schuster Children's Publishing Division
1230 Avenue of the Americas
New York, NY 10020

Book design by Lisa Vega
The text of this book was set in CenturyOldst BT.

Printed in the United States of America
6 8 10 9 7 5

Library of Congress Cataloging-in-Publication Data
Kurtz, Jane.
Johnny Appleseed / by Jane Kurtz ; illustrated by Mary Haverfield.
p. cm. — (Ready-to-read)
ISBN-13: 978-0-689-85959-5 (lib. ed.) — ISBN-13: 978-0-689-85958-8 (pbk.)
ISBN-10: 0-689-85959-7 (lib. ed.) — ISBN-10: 0-689-85958-9 (pbk.)
1. Appleseed, Johnny, 1774–1845—Juvenile literature.
2. Applegrowers—United States—Biography—Juvenile literature.
3. Frontier and pioneer life—Middle West—Juvenile literature.
[1. Appleseed, Johnny, 1774–1845. 2. Apple growers.
3. Frontier and pioneer life.] I. Haverfield, Mary, ill. II. Title. III. Series.
SB63.C46K87 2004
634'.11'092—dc22

2003024535

Johnny Appleseed

By Jane Kurtz

Illustrated by Mary Haverfield

Aladdin

New York   London   Toronto   Sydney

Who is that
walking by the Ohio?
Apple-loving Johnny.
Yes! Johnny Appleseed.

He carries a bag.

He carries a hoe.

He digs a hole
by his left big toe.

He drops a seed
into the hole.

He pat, pat, pats
the soft, black bed.

Soon the rains
will pitter-patter down,

and a green baby tree
will poke out
its little head.

Who is that
walking by the Ohio?

Apple-loving Johnny.
Yes! Johnny Appleseed.

He carries a bag
full of baby trees.

People ask,

"May I have one please?"

"What do you have
    to trade?" says he.

"Will you take a pan?"
"Yes."

"Will you take a ham?"
"Yes."

"Will you take a shirt?"
"Yes."

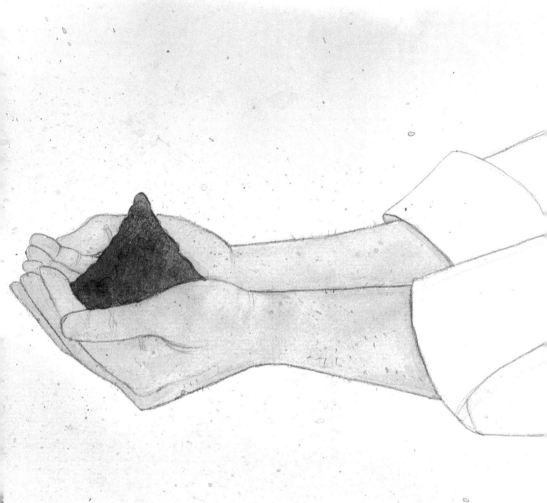

"Will you take some dirt?"

"Yes."

Who is that
walking by the Ohio?

Apple-loving Johnny.
Yes! Johnny Appleseed.

He hands something shiny
to a hopping girl.

The girl bites in
and says, "Oh! Sweet!"

Nobody cares
that his clothes are funny.
Nobody chuckles
at his big, bare feet.

They all work hard
with their plows
on their farms.

They get sore backs.
They get sore arms.

At the end of the day,
they can come inside

and bite into an apple

or a sweet apple pie.

Clap your hands for
Johnny.

Clap your hands for
Johnny Chapman.

Clap your hands for
Johnny Appleseed!